My New School

My New School:

A Workbook to Help Students Transition to a New School

Melissa L. Trautman, Ms. Ed.

Foreword by Brenda Smith Myles, Ph.D.

© 2010 Autism Asperger Publishing Co.
P.O. Box 23173
Shawnee Mission, Kansas 66283-0173
www.asperger.net

Publisher's Cataloging-in-Publication

Trautman, Melissa.

    My new school : a workbook to help students transition to a new school / Melissa L. Trautman. -- 1st ed. -- Shawnee Mission, Kan. : Autism Asperger Pub. Co., c2010.

        p. ; cm.
        ISBN: 978-1-934575-65-9
        LCCN: 2010921018
        Includes bibliographical references.

        1. Transfer students--United States--Handbooks, manuals, etc. 2. Students, Transfer of--United States--Handbooks, manuals, etc. 3. Student adjustment--Social aspects--United States. 4. School children--United States--Psychology. 5. Autism spectrum disorders--Patients--Education. 6. [Transfer students. 7. School adjustment.] I. Title.

LB3064.2 .T73 2010   2010921018
371.2/9140973--dc22   1003

This book is designed in Hobo and Franklin Gothic.

Cover illustration: ©istockphoto; Ratinoff Design

Interior illustrations ©istockphoto; doodlemachine.com

Printed in the United States of America.

Table of Contents

Foreword

Transitioning to a new school can be a harrowing experience for children and youth. For some of our children, the fear of the unknown can be almost debilitating. They become emotionally vulnerable in anticipation of the change, and may be on edge, melt down, cry, or become rigid or inflexible, making the transition even more difficult. This creates a vicious cycle, wherein the child or youth's anxiety continues to increase, in the process making the transition appear as an insurmountable barrier.

Research shows that priming – preparing the individual for an upcoming event – is an effective way to help plan for and experience a successful transition. Until now, there have been few materials designed to help a student prepare for what can be a very difficult transition – moving to new school.

In her comprehensive, yet easy-to-use book, Melissa Trautman helps children and youth understand all of the issues related to moving to a new school while empowering them to learn new skills, make a plan, and carry it out. *My New School: A Workbook to Help Students Transition to a New School* reflects best practice and practical solutions addressing issues such as schedules, lockers, lunchroom, and friendships. Successful transitions to a new school have just become easier with the help of this innovative book that is based on a deep insight into children and youth and their anxieties.

– Brenda Smith Myles, Ph.D., a consultant with the Ziggurat Group, is the recipient of the 2004 Autism Society of America's Outstanding Professional Award and the 2006 Princeton Fellowship Award. She has written numerous articles and books on Asperger Syndrome and autism, including *Asperger Syndrome and Difficult Moments: Practical Solutions for Tantrums, Rage, and Meltdowns* (with Southwick) and *Asperger Syndrome and Adolescence: Practical Solutions for School Success* (with Adreon). The latter is the winner of the Autism Society of America's 2002 Outstanding Literary Work.

Introduction

- Are you planning on moving to a new school?

- Are you getting worried or anxious about the move?

- Are you worried that you won't know anyone?

- Does your stomach hurt when you think about your new school?

If so, this book is for you!

This book is designed to help you with your worries. Moving to a new school will be hard, scary, and challenging, but you can do it! You will be O.K. and be able to settle in the new school successfully.

In this book we will discuss:
- Why you are moving schools
- Your current support system
- How to deal with your anxiety
- How to get information about your new school
- Who you are – your strengths and needs, and how you can share information about them with people at your new school
- What to do …
  - before school starts
  - the week before school starts
  - the first day of school
- Putting yourself out there and meeting new people
- Surviving the rest of the school year

My New School

As with any transition, you will need people to help you with the move to your new school. It will be important to have friends and adults to talk to about your worries and concerns. Your family and teachers at your current school will be important in this venture.

Any move is a process ... it cannot be done overnight. It will take time, and you will have many different feelings about the move. It is important to recognize how you are feeling throughout this process. All of your feelings about the move are O.K.

Take your time and be patient. Change is hard, but it can be a good thing. For example, moving to a new neighborhood may allow you to meet someone that will become your best friend. If you hadn't moved, then you would never have met your best friend!

Planning and talking about your new school will help ease your worry and concerns. Specifically, reading and completing the activities in this workbook will help you feel confident when you start at your new school. When you are ready, turn to the next page. You're about to start a new adventure!

Here are some quotes to get you thinking about change.

"Become a student of change. It is the only thing that will remain constant."
  – Anthony J. D'Angelo, Chief Visionary Officer of Collegiate EmPowerment

"Just because everything is different doesn't mean that everything has changed."
  – Irene Peter, American Author

"Change is the law of life. And those who look only to the past or present are certain to miss the future."
  – John F. Kennedy, 35th President of the United States of America

Please add any thoughts of your own about change:

_____

_____

Chapter 1
First Things First

Why are you moving to a new school?
(check which of these answers is correct)

☐ You are moving from elementary to middle school.

☐ You are moving from middle school to high school.

☐ Your family relocated.

☐ You and your family chose to move you to another school.

☐ Other reasons (write below):

_____

_____

_____

_____

My New School

Do you agree with the decision to move to another school? Are you happy or sad? Write down or draw a picture of your feelings regarding the move.

_____

_____

_____

_____

_____

_____

_____

First Things First

Hopefully, you have been a part of the decision to move. Some families have no choice but to move. They have to move because one of the parents is taking a new job, for example. Other families need to get a bigger or maybe a smaller house and, therefore, have to move.

No matter why you are moving, it is important to realize that at this point you can't change the reason why you are moving to another school. Your family has a specific reason why they decided to move. Even though you may not like it, the decision to start a new school has already been made.

If you are upset about the move and feel you weren't part of the decision, realize that it's O.K. to feel that way. Try to talk to your family and teachers about the decision calmly. Ask the following questions ...

1. Why are you moving to another school?
2. What are the reasons behind the decision to move?
3. Why does your family feel this move will be better for you?

After talking with your family, you may hear reasons that do not make much sense to you or reasons that you do not care about. Parents try to make decisions that are best for the entire family. Unless you are living your parents' lives, you may not understand the reason.

If you are still upset, try to create a list of positive things that may come out of the move. One positive might be that you will meet new friends. Another might be that you won't have to ride the bus to school.

It is sometimes hard to think positively, especially in a situation that you don't like. Ask your family or teachers at your school to help you think of positives that may come out of this move so you can focus on those.

We can't change the past, but we can always look forward to and change the future!

My New School

Now write or draw positive things that may come out of the move.

_____

_____

_____

_____

_____

_____

_____

Chapter 2
My Support System

It is important to be able to talk to friends and adults in your life about the upcoming transition. On this page, you will list people in your life that you can talk to about the move. You will also list people who can help you with this transition.

Family

_____

_____

_____

Teachers or School Staff

_____

_____

_____

Friends

_____

_____

_____

My New School

Now that you have listed the people in your support system, circle or highlight the names of two or three people in your family who will be the most helpful to you.

Then circle or highlight the names of two or three teachers or school staff who can help you with the transition to your new school.

Finally, circle or highlight the names of two or three friends that you can talk to and confide in about your worries or concerns about transitioning to your new school.

Remembering the people in your support system who can help you through this process will be important as you continue to work through your transition.

Chapter 3
How to Deal with My Anxiety

Anxiety can happen when you are placed into situations that are new to you, when your routine changes, or due to changes in your physical environment.

Moving to a new school will cause some anxiety because you will experience all these scenarios – you will be in situations that are new to you, your routine will change, and your physical environment will change.

You may be experiencing anxiety when you think about the move. You might feel your muscles tighten, your stomach might feel like you are getting sick, you might be breathing more quickly, or your palms might be getting sweaty. These are all normal reactions to anxiety.

Are there other feelings or signs that tell you that you are anxious or worried?

It's O.K. to be anxious about moving to a new school. You might feel like you don't even know where to start to deal with this major change. It's important for you to acknowledge your anxiety so that people in your support system can help you cope with the changes that will be coming in the next couple of months. This means talking to your parents, your siblings, or teachers that you trust – turn to the list you made up earlier on page 7.

My New School

Sometimes it seems easier to just try to forget events that make you anxious and think about something that you really enjoy. But if you do that and don't really think about what you are feeling or what is making you nervous, the move to a new school will be extremely difficult. It's important to know how you feel and what makes you anxious. That is the first step in dealing with your anxiety.

To help you sort out your feelings related to the upcoming move, you are now going to complete an activity where you assign numbers to your feelings, in order of intensity. We will be using a scale ranging from 1 to 5 based on the book *The Incredible 5-Point Scale* by Kari Dunn Buron and Mitzi Curtis.

When using a 5-point scale, each number is labeled to explain a feeling or anxiety that you may have during a certain situation. The numbers and the matching feelings are listed below as they may apply to your transition to a new school.

1 = I can handle this. I'm O.K.

2 = This might make me feel uncomfortable, but I will still try it.

3 = This could make me really nervous. I might need someone to help prepare me for this situation ahead of time.

4 = This could make me feel sick to my stomach or extremely nervous. I will need some help during this situation to make it through.

5 = There is no way that I will be able to handle this situation.

In the Appendix, you will find a 5-point scale that you can use with these categories printed on it. The Appendix also includes cards with situations listed on them. In addition, blank cards are provided where you can write other situations that are specific to your transition; for example, classes or school events that have been hard in the past.

Together with someone in your support system (parent, teachers, etc.), sort the cards according to how you would feel in the situation described. For instance, keeping in mind the 5-point scale, eating in the lunchroom in your new school might be a "3." Meeting new people might be a "5." Or maybe it's the other way around.

Remember that these situations often cause different feelings for different people going through a transition. It's O.K. if you put a situation in the "1" category and someone else going through the same transition puts it in the "4" category on their scale.

How to Deal with My Anxiety

After sorting the cards, write on the card the number of the category you placed it in. Then collect all the cards that you put in your "4" and "5" categories. Write down on a list the cards that you placed in these categories so you can refer to it after your visits to your new school see if your concerns were addressed (see page 12).

Talk with your support person about ways to help deal with the situations listed on the cards in your "4" and "5" categories. It is important to start with cards in the top two categories (4 and 5) since those situations cause you the most anxiety. After discussing and dealing with your "4's" and "5's," you can address the rest of your concerns in the "3," "2," and "1" categories. Sharing these concerns with staff at your new school will help them know about situations that would provoke anxiety for you.

You might already have strategies that you use to help deal with your anxiety. If you do, that's great! It's important to have those strategies in your life. Don't forget to use them during this transition. If you are unsure of how to deal with your anxiety, don't worry. Strategies to help deal with anxiety are discussed in Chapter 9.

5-Point Scale Card Sort

Name: _____

Cards in "4" Category

This could make me feel sick to my stomach or extremely nervous. I will need some help during this situation to make it through.

Cards in "5" Category

There is no way that I will be able to handle this situation.

Chapter 4
Who I Am

In this section of the workbook, you will think about what you like about school, what you don't like about school; things that you do well and things that you can improve upon.

It is important to know your thoughts about school so that you can share that information with people at your new school!

You are going to write down your favorite subjects in school, your least favorite subjects, things that you do well, and things that you are working on. It is also important to think about your daily schedule, what type of teacher makes you the most comfortable, any accommodations teachers can use to help you, and your anxiety and fears about school.

Information about you outside of school is also important to share. You will write down some of your favorite things to do when you are at home, what your family is like, your friends, and any other information that you want to share with teachers.

To prepare for one of your visits to your new school, your support person can help you make copies of the Who I Am Profile to bring to help introduce yourself to your new teachers and other school staff.

Who I Am Profile

Name _____   Grade _____

My Favorite Subjects in School (check as many as appropriate)

☐ Math   ☐ Reading   ☐ Writing   ☐ Social studies

☐ Science   ☐ PE   ☐ Art   ☐ Music

☐ Computers   ☐ Other: _____   ☐ Other:_____   ☐ Other:_____

My Least Favorite Subjects in School (check as many as appropriate)

☐ Math   ☐ Reading   ☐ Writing   ☐ Social studies

☐ Science   ☐ PE   ☐ Art   ☐ Music

☐ Computers   ☐ Other: _____   ☐ Other:_____   ☐ Other:_____

The Type of Teacher I Like to Work With ... (check as many as appropriate)

☐ Is a male   ☐ Is very structured (follows through on rules)   ☐ Maintains a quiet classroom

☐ Is a female   ☐ Doesn't talk very much   ☐ Allows kids to talk in the classroom

☐ Has a soft voice   ☐ Has a sense of humor   ☐ Is flexible

☐ Has a loud voice   ☐ Tells me what we are doing before we start on a given day   ☐ Other:_____

☐ Uses a lot of visuals (notes, writing on the board, overhead, etc.) when talking   ☐ Doesn't change the order of what we do every day   ☐ Other:_____

Accommodations That Help Me (check as many as appropriate)

☐ Preferential seating   ☐ Visuals (notes on boards, videos, pictures)

☐ Copies of notes   ☐ Extra time on long-term projects

☐ Use of calculator in math   ☐ Different setting for tests

☐ Breaking assignments into smaller parts   ☐ Study guide for tests

☐ Reduced number of problems assigned   ☐ Other: _____

☐ Rephrasing a concept if needed   ☐ Other: _____

☐ Repeat directions   ☐ Other: _____

Who I Am

Subjects That I Would Prefer to Take in the Morning *(check as many as appropriate)*

☐ Math   ☐ Reading

☐ Science   ☐ Communication arts (writing)

☐ Social studies   ☐ Other:_____   ☐ Other:_____

Subjects That I Would Prefer to Take in the Afternoons
(check as many as appropriate)

☐ Math   ☐ Reading

☐ Science   ☐ Communication arts (writing)

☐ Social studies   ☐ Other:_____   ☐ Other:_____

Things I Do Well _____

Things I Am Working On _____

Part(s) of My Day That Cause(s) the Most Anxiety or Worry for Me
(check as many as appropriate)

☐ Math   ☐ Communication arts (writing)

☐ Science   ☐ Passing periods between classes

☐ Social studies   ☐ Exploratory class (for example, art, computers, industrial technology, drama)

☐ Reading   ☐ Homework

☐ Lunch   ☐ Organizing my books and papers

☐ PE   ☐ Arrival at school

☐ Other:_____   ☐ Other:_____

Transportation to School Will Be By *(check as many as appropriate)*

☐ School bus   ☐ Carpool   ☐ Other:_____

☐ Parents   ☐ Walking   ☐ Other:_____

Transportation From School Will Be By *(check as many as appropriate)*

☐ School bus   ☐ Carpool   ☐ Other:_____

☐ Parents   ☐ Walking   ☐ Other:_____

My New School

My Family Consists Of (list names)

_____

_____

When I Get Home From School, I Like To (check as many as appropriate)

☐ Take a break
☐ Do homework
☐ Other

My Favorite Things to Do at Home (check as many as appropriate)

☐ Play video games ☐ Read books ☐ Play board games

☐ Talk to my friends ☐ Watch TV ☐ Be with my family

☐ Go outside ☐ Other:_____

☐ Play with my pets ☐ Other:_____

Other Information I Would Like to Share With My New School
(add any specific sensory needs you may have, such as loud noises, overhead lighting,
tight spaces, etc.):

_____

_____

_____

_____

_____

_____

Sometimes moving to a new school can be made easier if your new teachers know about your previous school schedule. They might also want to know if you had any special supports during the school day. The chart on page 18, known as the comprehensive planning system (CPS), is one way to let your teachers know what your previous school day looked like. Filling out the CPS chart is not hard, but if you need help, you can ask a parent or teacher.

Here is how you complete the chart.

Columns 1 (Time) & 2 (Activity): Fill in the time and the name of all of your classes. Use one line per class.

Column 3 (Targeted Skills to Teach): Leave this column blank. Your teacher can fill this in, if he wishes.

Column 4 (Structure/Modifications): Supports and modifications are special types of assistance that you may use to make your class a bit easier. Here are some examples of supports: (a) a written or picture schedule, (b) taking a test in another class, (c) completing fewer problems than other students, (d) a homework planner or to-do list, (e) a copy of lecture notes from the teacher or another student so that you can listen to a lecture without having to write, and (f) typing assignments instead of writing them by hand. For each class written down, list the types of help, supports, or modifications you used. If you do not have special supports or modifications for a specific class, just leave that line blank. Write all supports and modifications for one class on one line next to the Time and Activity.

Column 5 (Reinforcement): Reinforcement is extra recognition of your accomplishments for something that you have done that is kind of difficult. This reinforcement usually does not occur all the time. In fact, you may leave this area blank. Or you may have a token economy where you earn stickers or tokens for your behavior, turning in homework, completing assignments in class, or paying attention. You might also earn computer time after you complete assignments. Or perhaps you worked to earn lunchtime with your teacher. If any of this applies to you, for each class, write down what kind of reinforcement you received.

Column 6 (Sensory Supports): Many students have sensory challenges – sometimes things are too loud or there are too many things going on around you. You may become stressed out and don't know how to calm down. Your teacher or occupational therapist might have helped you by giving you some sensory supports, such as (a) a fidget, (b) a disco seat, (c) a chance to walk around or run an errand, (d) a cool-down spot (sometimes called a home base), (d) gum to chew, (e) early release from one class to go to another, (f) an Incredible 5-Point Scale, or (g) a special break. If you have sensory supports, write down the type of supports you had for each class. You may not have any sensory supports or only have some for one or two classes.

Column 7 (Communication/Social Skills): It is common for students to get help in talking and interacting with others. You may have (a) a conversation starter card that you use at lunch, (b) a reminder card that tells you to raise your hand before talking in class, (c) a Social Story™ that describes how to handle new situations, (d) a help card that you can place on your desk to show the teacher that you need help, and (e) a hidden curriculum calendar or a Mac App that you use each day to learn about unwritten rules. You may also have a social skills class where you have to keep a list of social skills as you use them. Write down the communication and social skills supports that you have for each class. If you don't have any communication or social supports for a class, leave that part blank.

Columns 8 (Data Collection) and 9 (Generalization): Do not complete these columns. If they are used (and they might not be), they should be completed by an adult.

After you have completed the CPS, you will have your schedule for the day and all of the supports that have helped you be successful. This will help teachers in your new school plan your schedule and make sure that you get what you need to be successful.

Comprehensive Planning System (CPS)

Child/Student: _____

1	2	3	4	5	6	7	8	9
Time	Activity	Targeted Skills to Teach	Structure/ Modifications	Reinforcement	Sensory Strategies	Communication/ Social Skills	Data Collection	Generalization Plan
8:00-8:50	Reading	Teacher can complete or leave blank	• Homework Planner checked by teacher • 1/2 problems • Quiet area for tests	• Token economy for turning in homework	• Walk before tests • Fidget	• Card to prompt to ask for help	Teacher can complete or leave blank	Teacher can complete or leave blank

Henry, S. A., & Myles, B. S. (2007). *Integrating best practices throughout the student's daily schedule: The Comprehensive Autism Planning System (CAPS) for individuals with Asperger Syndrome, autism and related disabilities.* Shawnee Mission, KS: Autism Asperger Publishing Company. Used with permission.

Chapter 5
My New School

It is important to gather as much information as you can about your new school. Such information will help answer some of the questions you may have and help ease your anxiety.

In this age of technology, almost every school district has a website. You can get a lot of information from your new school's website. Otherwise, they may have brochures and other materials with information about the school.

Let's play detective and find out some of the information that you want to know about your new school.

(You may need help from an adult or friend in your support system to find some of this information.)

My New School

The name of my new school is:_____

Here is a picture of my new school!

(Print off a picture of your new school and paste it here.)

The mascot of my new school is the: _____

More Information About My New School

My new principal's name is _____.

(circle the correct answer)

My new school has an assistant principal.	Yes	No
My new school has counselors to help students.	Yes	No
My new school offers my favorite subject.	Yes	No
My new school offers at least one exploratory class that I am interested in (examples: choir, band, speech, drama, art, industrial tech, foods class).	Yes	No
My new school offers at least one extracurricular activity that I am interested in.	Yes	No

Overall, my impressions about my new school are: *(check)*

☐ It looks very bad.
☐ It doesn't look good.
☐ It's O.K.
☐ It looks good!
☐ I'm very excited!

Chapter 6
Before School Starts

There are many things that you can do to help you become comfortable with the transition to your new school. In this chapter are activities for you and adults in your support system to complete before it is time to start your new school.

Take each activity one at a time. Talk with the adults in your support system about when you can do some of these activities. You don't need to do every activity. Do as many as it takes to make you feel comfortable before the first day of school.

When you complete the activities, it is important to write down what happened, your feelings and thoughts about the activity, and how you think it will help you the first day of school. Processing the activities like this will help reduce some of the anxiety that you are feeling about the transition.

Feel free to add to or change any activity listed to help your transition to your new school go as smoothly as possible. For example, you may want to ask people in your support system if they have any other ideas or activities for you to do before school starts. There are extra activity sheets at the end of the chapter to use if you have another idea or activity that you think will be helpful for you to do.

Activity #1 – Visiting My New School

Pay a visit to your new school with someone from your support system. This may be a teacher at school or your parents. The purpose of this visit is to walk through the school and get comfortable in the building. It is a good idea to visit before or after school when there are not many students and staff in the building. You will meet students and staff during other visits to the school. During this particular visit, the adult who came with you may introduce himself or herself to the principal. You may want to bring your camera to take pictures of your new school.

Copy this page or take your workbook with you so you can follow and check off your to-do list during the visit.

Date I'm going to visit _____

I am going with _____.

To-Do List During My Visit

(check)

☐ Find the school office.

☐ Introduce myself to the secretary to let the new school know I am there.

☐ Ask for a map of the school.

☐ Allow members of my support system time to talk with the principal. If I feel comfortable, I will introduce myself to the principal.

☐ Walk around the hallways and look at a locker.

☐ Look into a classroom.

☐ Look at the locker rooms and the gym.

☐ Use the map to find the following places:

__ The nurse's office and the counselor's office

__ The lunchroom

__ The restrooms

__ Exploratory classrooms

There may be other rooms or places in your new school that you want to check out. That's good! Take your time visiting your new school.

What I Learned During the Visit

When you come back from your visit, answer the following questions.

1. What happened on the visit?

2. What are my feelings and thoughts about the visit?

3. How will the information I learned during the visit help me the first day of school?

Students or Staff Members Whom I Met During My Visit

Name	How Will I Remember Them?

(Attach a map of your new school here.)

Activity #2 – Meeting a Support Person at My New School

Copy the Who I Am Profile on pages 14-16 and bring it with you on this visit!

Find a support person at your new school. If possible, set up a time to meet with a staff member from your new school before school starts. You can ask one of your teachers or parents to help you with this. This could be the principal, a school counselor, or a teacher that you will be working with. You may want to bring a camera to take a picture of this person.

Copy this page or take your workbook with you so you can follow and check off your to-do list during the visit.

Date I'm going to visit _____

I am going with _____.

I am going to meet:

_____   _____
           Name   Position

_____   _____
           Name   Position

To-Do List During My Visit

(check)

☐ Introduce myself to the person that I am meeting with.

☐ Ask questions about my new school.

☐ Give my new support person my Who I Am Profile.

☐ Discuss my strengths and needs and what my new school can do to help me.

☐ Bring camera or cell phone with camera or ask for pictures of staff I meet.

How the Visit Went

I feel that my visit went ... *(check)*

☐ Not so good. I'm not sure if I can trust staff at my new school.
☐ Just O.K. I still need to spend more time with staff at my new school.
☐ Great! I feel like I can trust the new staff at my new school.

What I Learned During the Visit

It's O.K. if your first visit with a staff member at your new school does not go as well as you wanted it to. Remember that you will be working with a lot of different staff members and teachers. If you feel you aren't comfortable with the staff member you met, ask someone in your support system to help you set up another visit with another staff member at the school.

It is important for you to have someone you trust and that you can talk to when you start your new school!

Below, jot down any notes, impressions, or suggestions that the staff member at your new school gave you that will help the transition to your new school go smoothly.

_____

_____

_____

_____

_____

_____

_____

Students or Staff Members Whom I Met During My Visit

Name	How Will I Remember Them?

Photo Album

(Use this page to tape pictures of the staff you meet at your new school. Be sure to list their names and position in the school.)

Activity #3 – Visiting the Lunchroom

Try to visit the lunchroom of your new school during the school day. It's important to learn how to navigate the lunchroom, where to sit, and rules of the lunchroom.

Ask one of the adults in your support system to help set up a lunch visit. During the visit, staff at your new school may be able to introduce you to other students in the school that you can eat lunch with.

Lunchroom visits can be stressful. Lunchrooms are usually noisy, loud, and crowded. It is important for you to find out what the lunchroom is like so that you will be comfortable the first day of school. You may want to bring a camera to take a picture of the lunchroom setup.

It's O.K. if you don't feel comfortable in the lunchroom during this first visit. It's also O.K. if you don't want to stay the entire time. Talk with the person from your support system who is going with you. Develop a plan for what to do if you want to leave. Write down your plan now before you visit.

My plan if I want to leave early from the lunchroom is to:

Copy this page and the to-do list or take your workbook with you so you can follow and check off your to-do list during the visit.

Date I'm going to visit _____

I am going with _____.

To-Do List During My Lunchroom Visit

Sitting Down in the Lunchroom

(circle the appropriate answer)

Do the students have assigned seats?	Yes	No
Do the students sit wherever they want?	Yes	No
Can students save seats for each other?	Yes	No
Do students get their lunch first and then sit down?	Yes	No
How many students can sit at a table?	_____	

Going Through the Lunch Line

Is there a line I need to get into for lunch?	Yes	No
Can I choose to eat anything I want at lunch?	Yes	No
Do I need a lunch account number?	Yes	No

Eating and the End of Lunch Time

Is a table cleaner assigned daily?	Yes	No
Can I get up and clean off my tray any time I want?	Yes	No

Students or Staff Members Whom I Met in the Lunchroom

Name	How Will I Remember Them?

What I Learned During My Visit

When you come back from your visit, answer the following questions.

1. What happened on my visit to the lunchroom?

2. What are my feelings and thoughts about the lunchroom?

3. How will this visit to the lunchroom help me the first day of school?

Activity #4 – Locker and Schedule

Check out your locker and schedule. About 1 to 2 weeks before school starts, you will probably want to go up to your new school to get your locker combination and your schedule.

It is important to get your locker combination so that you can start practicing and memorizing your combination. It will help you on the first day of school if you can find and get into your locker easily. So practice!

You will also feel less anxious about coming to school on the first day if you know your schedule. It is important to get your schedule so that you can become familiar with it.

Having these two things completed before school starts will help you relax on the first day of your new school!

Date I'm going to visit _____

I am going with _____.

My locker number is #_____.

My locker combination is _____-_____-_____.

When you get your schedule ...
(check)
☐ Figure out how to read your schedule (which class comes first, second, etc.).
☐ Find the room number for each class.
☐ Use the map that you received (see page 27) earlier to find your classrooms.
☐ Once you have found all of your classrooms, return to your locker.
☐ Start at your locker and walk through your entire schedule.
☐ Practice several times so that you know what rooms you will need to go to.

Before School Starts

After you feel comfortable walking your schedule through the building, make sure to take the copy of your schedule with you. You may want to retype or write out an easier schedule for you to understand. You can put it on another piece of paper or an index card if it is easier to carry. You may also want to Velcro your schedule inside the cover of your textbooks or in your locker. Remember to practice and memorize your locker combination also!

Here is an example of how to write out an easy-to-read schedule.

Hour	Time	Class	Room	Teacher
1	7:45 – 8:30	Science	213	Mr. Smith
2	8:35 – 9:20	Math	216	Mrs. Weimer
3	9:25-10:10	Reading	208	Mr. Jones
4	10:15 -11:00	Art	145	Ms. Johnson
Lunch	11:00 – 11:35		Lunchroom	
5	11:40 – 12:20	Music	135	Mr. Barth
6	12:25 – 1:10	Social Studies	211	Mrs. Little
7	1:15 – 2:00	Study Hall	200	Mrs. Toones

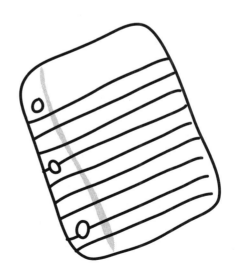

(Attach your schedule here.)

Activity #_____

(Activity)

Date I'm going to visit _____

I am going with _____.

To-Do List

☐ _____

☐ _____

☐ _____

☐ _____

☐ _____

☐ _____

☐ _____

When you come back from your visit, answer the following questions.

1. What happened on the visit?

2. What are my feelings and thoughts about the visit?

3. How will the visit help me the first day of school?

Activity #_____

(Activity)

Date I'm going to visit _____

I am going with _____.

To-Do List

☐ _____

☐ _____

☐ _____

☐ _____

☐ _____

☐ _____

☐ _____

When you come back from your visit, answer the following questions.

1. What happened on the visit?

2. What are my feelings and thoughts about the visit?

3. How will the visit help me the first day of school?

Chapter 7
The Week Before School

The first day of school can cause a lot of anxiety and stress, especially at a new school. There are several things that you can do to help relieve or lessen your stress and anxiety. Many of them should begin the week before school actually starts. Try to do as many as you can ahead of time, so you aren't rushing the morning that school starts.

Remember, preparation is the best strategy to prevent stress and anxiety!

To-Do List for the Week Before School Starts

(check)

☐ Supplies: Get the supply list from the school office and buy your school supplies. The office secretary usually has copies of the supply list for every grade, or you can look on the school's website. Some local stores, such as Walmart, have school supply lists from schools in the area.

☐ You should have your locker combination and locker number at this point (see page 36). Ask someone from your support system to drive you to your new school so you can put your supplies in your new locker. Schools are typically open during normal school hours the month before school starts. You may want to call the school office to check to see when they are open.

☐ Buy the backpack that you will use at your new school or get out the one you already have.

☐ Check into PE clothing. Some schools require that you purchase specific clothing to be worn during PE class. Ask the school secretary or your support staff at your new school about PE clothes; ask the secretary for an order form or check on the school's website for more information and/or a printable order form.

☐ Practice getting up in the mornings at the time you will have to get up when school starts.

☐ Practice getting ready for school and eating breakfast so you know how much time it will take you.

To-Do List for the Night Before School Starts

(check)

☐ Pack your backpack with any supplies that you may need on the first day of school.

☐ Set out the outfit that you will wear the first day of school.

☐ Pack your lunch if you are not going to eat in the lunchroom.

☐ Review your schedule and your locker combination.

And finally …

☐ Go to bed early and get some sleep!

Tomorrow will be a good day because I am prepared!

Chapter 8
The First Day of School

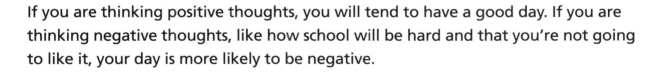

When you wake up for the first day of going to your new school, tell yourself that everything will be O.K. and that you will have a good school year. It is important to think positive thoughts any time you go into a new situation. You can think about the new friends that you will make, the new teachers that you'll meet, and the new support people that you already have at the school.

If you are thinking positive thoughts, you will tend to have a good day. If you are thinking negative thoughts, like how school will be hard and that you're not going to like it, your day is more likely to be negative.

To-Do List for the Morning School Starts

(check)

☐ Wake up at the time that you practiced the week before.

☐ Get dressed and ready.

☐ Eat breakfast.

☐ Get your backpack and lunch box (if needed).

☐ Review your schedule and your locker combination one more time.

☐ On your way to school, tell yourself one more time that today will be O.K. and that you are going to have a good school year. Remember – positive thoughts!

☐ Arrive at school 10-15 minutes early. This will give you time to find your locker again and try to relax before your first class.

Things to Remember on My First Day of School

- You don't have to do everything perfect the first day of school. If you need help with something, or if you forget where to go on your schedule, ask a teacher.

- On the first day, teachers usually talk about the rules of the classroom, the extra supplies you might need, and any homework that you may have.

- There may be an assembly or a grade-level activity the first day of school. Be aware that the schedule may be different.

- If you get stressed or anxious during the day, ask the teacher if you can take a break or go see one of the staff members that you have previously visited.

- It's O.K. if things change on the first day of school. Sometimes schedules have to change due to the number of kids in the classrooms or other reasons you may not be aware of.

- Look around at the kids in your classes. You may notice that some of them are in several of your classes.

- Don't be afraid to talk to other students in your classrooms at the appropriate times. Introduce yourself and ask what their names are. Write their names down if you think you won't remember them later.

- Remember – this is just the first day at your new school. If it doesn't go as well as you wanted, that's O.K. Tomorrow is another day!

Chapter 9
Putting Myself out There! How to Meet New People

Starting a new school can be very difficult socially, especially if you are new to the area. It's important to have friends in your support system that you can talk to or eat lunch with.

This new adventure might be difficult, especially if you have a hard time introducing yourself to new people.

Some of your concerns about meeting new friends might be:
- Introducing yourself
- Finding common interests to talk about
- Finding time to talk with your new friends
- Thinking that no one will like you

Perhaps you have other concerns. If so, write them here.

_____

_____

_____

Let's look at some ways to deal with social challenges like this.

Introducing Myself

There are many ways to introduce yourself. It is important to learn how to introduce yourself in new social situations. Listed below are a couple of ways to introduce yourself to someone new. Role-play these situations with someone in your support system before going to your new school.

Choice #1 (from *Super Skills* by Judith Coucouvanis)
1. Smile.
2. Look at the person.
3. Say: "Hi, my name is _____. What's your name?"
4. Listen to the answer and say, "Hi, _____. It's nice to meet you."

Choice #2 (from *Social Skills Training* by Jed Baker)
1. Decide if this is a person you want to meet.
2. Try to get the person's attention with a gesture or by saying, "Excuse me."
3. Make eye contact and use a strong, positive tone of voice.
4. Say, "My name is _____. What's your name?"
5. Then say, "It's nice to meet you."

Choice #3
1. Walk up to the person you want to meet.
2. Make eye contact.
3. Say, "Hey, I'm _____. What's your name?"
4. Then say, "Nice to meet you."

Finding Common Interests to Talk About

After you have introduced yourself to a possible new friend, find out what his or her interests are. It's O.K. to have friends who are not interested in the same activities as you are, but it's also important to find friends who are interested in some of the same activities. It gives you something to talk about right away.

Ways to Find out What Other Students' Interests Are

- Listen to what they say they do on the weekends.
- Look at what they are reading.
- Find out if they are involved in any after-school activities by asking if they know anything about the after-school activities at the school.
- Watch in the classroom to see if they contribute to conversations about a certain subject.
- Be observant – often other students draw pictures or write on their notebooks about things that they are interested in.

Finding Time to Talk to Your New Friends

When you start a new school, you might be more worried about homework and trying to get used to the new school environment than about making friends. That's O.K. Take your time doing those things.

Once you have started to find students with whom you have things in common, it is important to find time to talk. This will allow you to get to know them better and feel more comfortable around them. This is how friendships start.

Here are some times when you can talk to your friends:
- Passing periods
- Lunch time
- Before school
- After school
- In the classroom before the bell rings
- At the end of class when the teacher has finished teaching – if allowed!

Be careful if you are talking to your friends during class time. Be sure to keep an eye on the teacher and stop talking when it's time to start class. You don't want to get in trouble with the teacher for talking during class!

Other Times When You Can Talk to Your New Friends

It's important to try to get involved in some sort of activity at your new school to meet other students and make new friends. This could be in the school play, computer club, chess club, athletics, community service club, or any other club or group that interests you.

For some students, staying after school another hour or two is stressful because they are already tired and just want a break. It's O.K. to feel that way, but if you want to make friends, you will need to make an effort to get involved in something.

If you feel you just can't get involved in an after-school activity, talk with your school counselor. She may know of groups that meet at lunch time or during the school day that you can get involved in. If your school counselor does not have any ideas for groups to join, talk to her about your situation and how hard it is for you to meet new students. Most school counselors are more than willing to try to help students find new friends and times to talk with them.

Possible After-School Activities

Here are some after-school activities that may be available at your school. Check with your new support person, look around at flyers posted on the walls, or ask the secretary about the types of activities your school offers.

- Chess Club
- Computer Club
- Sports (volleyball, football, basketball, track)
- School Play (acting)
- School Play (backstage or tech support)
- Community Service Club
- Debate Club
- Art Club

Do any of these activities interest you? If so, talk to your support person at school or the school secretary to find out where and when the after-school activity meets. Write down the information you gather on the form on page 51.

Possible After-School Activities

After-School Activity	When Does it Meet?	Who Is in Charge?	How Long Does It Meet After School?	Do I Need to Bring Anything to Participate?

Before committing to any after-school activity, make sure to talk with your parents to see if it is O.K. Some schools do not provide transportation for after-school activities, so your parents may have to develop a plan to pick you up after your activity is over.

What About My Old Friends?

Students who move to a different neighborhood or a new school often worry about their friends at their old school. With the use of technology, it is much easier to stay friends with people after you move away. If you would like to stay friends, it's important that you take the time to visit or communicate with your old friends.

Staying in Touch

Here are some suggestions for how to stay in touch with your old friends. Make sure to talk with your family, especially when dealing with computer email and Facebook accounts. Have an adult help you set privacy settings so only your friends can access your information online.

- Text your friends using your cell phone (make sure to ask your parents so you don't accumulate extra charges on your cell phone bill).
- Skype (calling your friends over your computer) your friends. Go to www. skype.com for more information on how to use Skype.

- Start an email or Facebook account so you can stay in touch with your friends.
- Set a monthly date to get together with your friends. For example, every second Friday of the month can be movie night, where you go to a movie with your old friends.
- Call your old friends if you miss talking to them or need advice.

Sometimes, time and distance become too much, and people you were friends with at your old school do not stay as close of friends as before. This may be due to two people not having enough time to talk, their interests becoming different, or becoming friends with other people in their school.

If you are sad or depressed about missing your friends from your old school, talk to your family or your support system at your new school. They will have ideas to help you deal with your feelings.

Chapter 10
Surviving the Rest of the School Year

Three specific areas need to be addressed for you to have a successful year at your new school. The first is anxiety. It will be important for you to develop strategies to deal with your anxiety so you are able to stay calm and not be nervous about being at school.

The second area is "self-advocacy" and learning how to learn to advocate for yourself. Self-advocacy is a time-intensive process that usually takes years to complete. This chapter will provide some ideas to start learning how to advocate for yourself.

The third area is knowing the "hidden curriculum" of your new school. This is also very important to settling into your new school as well as life beyond school.

Anxiety

When your anxiety increases during the new school year, it will be important to have strategies to help relax and/or calm you down. You may experience anxiety when situations occur that you aren't ready for or when your classes start introducing new material. On the next page is a list of strategies that you can try during the first couple of weeks of school. If you need help implementing these strategies, let someone in your new support system know so they can help.

Strategies for Reducing Anxiety

- Take a deep breath and count to 10.
- Get a drink of water.
- Take a short walk down the hall or to a designated spot. Make sure to let an adult in the classroom know that you are leaving and where you are going.
- Read a book.
- Go to a quiet place that has been arranged ahead of time with your teachers. Stay until you are calm.
- Talk to someone about what is making you anxious.
- Draw a picture.
- Think about something that you like to do or enjoy.
- Write in a journal.
- Use a fidget or stress ball.
- Listen to music.

Different classrooms and situations may require different strategies. Listening to music in reading class, for instance, may not be appropriate, but reading something of special interest for a couple of minutes might be O.K. by the teacher. It's important to find a strategy that will help you when you become anxious but that is acceptable within the class or other school situation. You may want to Velcro a card in your textbook or class notebook to remind you what to do when you are anxious because it is sometimes difficult to remember what to do when you are feeling stressed.

Each teacher has different rules and suggestions for their classrooms. It is important to talk to your teachers ahead of time about strategies that you can use when you are stressed. Ask your parents or support staff in your new school to help you talk with your new teachers if you feel uncomfortable doing it yourself.

Another strategy that will help you survive the rest of the school year is to find teachers or other staff that you feel comfortable with and that you can trust. Trustworthy adults are individuals who won't judge what you tell them or hold what you tell them against you. They understand your specific needs and accommodations that will help you, and they enjoy spending time with you.

It may take a couple of weeks to find those people in your new school. The teachers and staff that you spent time with and visited at the beginning of your transition are great people to start with. Continue to talk with those people to build your relationship and trust. Building your new support system in your new school is important so you have people that you can turn to.

Advocate for Yourself

Think back to Activity #2 on pages 28-31 when you visited a new staff person at your school. The purpose of that activity was to help start a relationship with a staff member at your new school who could become your support person. It is important to have someone at school who believes in you and can be part of your support system when you need help and support.

Along with finding your new support system, it is important to learn to advocate for yourself. Advocating for yourself involves telling your friends or your teachers exactly what you need to be successful. Share with your new teachers things that they can do to help you be the best that you can be. Advocating for yourself is a process where you will learn a lot about yourself.

This process does not come naturally. It will take a lot of effort and time, probably years, to become a good advocate for yourself. Throughout this workbook, we have asked you to start advocating for yourself in small ways. Filling out the Who I Am Profile and sharing that profile with your support person at your new school is an example of advocating for yourself. Also, talking to teachers about strategies to use to calm down at the beginning of this chapter is advocating for yourself.

Ways to Become a Self-Advocate

Here are some other activities that will get you started to learn to advocate for yourself. Check off any activities that you plan to try or ones that you have already completed.
- Copy the Who I Am Profile on page 14 and pass it out to all of the teachers that you see throughout your school day.
- Type up suggestions for how teachers can help you in class.
- Develop a PowerPoint presentation about yourself, discussing your strengths and needs and share it with your teachers.

- If you have a hard time with handwriting, ask your teachers to let you use a computer to type your papers.
- Ask for a quiet place to work if the classroom gets too loud for you to concentrate in.

A great resource to learn how to advocate for yourself is *The Integrated Self-Advocacy Curriculum – A Program for Emerging Self-Advocates with Autism Spectrum and Other Conditions* by Valerie Paradiz and *Ask and Tell: Self-Advocacy and Disclosure for People on the Autism Spectrum,* edited by Stephen Shore. You can also work through *Asperger Syndrome: An Owner's Manual: What You, Your Parents and Your Teachers Need to Know* and *Asperger Syndrome: An Owner's Manual 2 For Older Adolescents and Adults – What You, Your Parents and Friends, and Your Employer, Need to Know* both written by Ellen S. Heller Korin. All of these books provide great information on what advocacy is and how to become an advocate for yourself.

Hidden Curriculum

Every school has a hidden curriculum or "hidden rules" that are never told to students, but the teachers and staff expect them to be followed. Hidden rules can also exist among students. If you have difficulty with social situations already, the hidden curriculum can be extremely hard to figure out.

Examples of the Hidden Curriculum

Here are some examples of the hidden curriculum in a school environment taken from *The Hidden Curriculum* by Myles, Trautman, and Schelvan.

- Even though you might have every answer or part of a project correct, teachers usually also grade you on neatness.
- It's O.K. to hang out in the hallway and talk with friends up until the bell rings.
- Talk to your teacher in a different way than you talk to your friends. Always use a polite voice when speaking with a teacher.
- While it might be O.K. to use profanity in private, it is not appropriate to do so in public, especially when adults are near.
- It's O.K. to tell jokes and share funny comments at lunch time, but it's not okay to tell inappropriate jokes.
- It's O.K. to write on your own notebooks and papers, but it's not okay to write on someone else's notebooks or papers.

It is important to learn the hidden curriculum at your new school. Talk with your new support staff and/or the speech-language pathologist. Ask them to share with you the "hidden" rules of your new school. If you find a student that you feel you can trust, ask him or her about the rules of the school that teachers usually don't share with you directly. Learning the hidden curriculum will help you fit in better and make you feel more comfortable in your new environment.

Here are some activities that you can do to help you become familiar with the hidden curriculum at your new school. Check off any activity that you are interested in doing or that you complete.

Activities to Help Become Familiar with the Hidden Curriculum

☐ Buy a One-a-Day Hidden Curriculum calendar; available at Autism Asperger Publishing Company (http://www.asperger.net). Hidden curriculum rules are now also available as a Mac App (go to www.iTunes.com or the App Store on your iPhone or iPod touch). Read the calendar daily and discuss the hidden curriculum item with your parents or other adults.

☐ Read a book targeted towards kids. A great book on unwritten rules for teenagers is *How Rude! The Teenager's Guide to Good Manners, Proper Behavior, and Not Grossing People Out* by Alex J. Packer.

☐ Start a notebook where you write down all of the unwritten rules that you notice throughout the day. Keep it at school in a special place where you can get at it if you encounter one of these unwritten rules. When you start really paying attention to examples of the hidden curriculum, you will find that the "rules" depend on such factors as your age, whether you are a boy or a girl, where you are, etc. There are two forms on the following pages – a blank diary for you to fill in and discuss with your parents and teachers and a sample diary giving you an idea of what to look for.

☐ Go to a trusted adult or support staff at school and ask them to watch situations in school to see if you are missing any hidden curriculum items.

My Hidden Curriculum Diary – Sample

Age	By the time I am age 12, people expect that I can cut my own food when I am eating. People might think you are "weird" if you play with little toys if you are a teenager.
Place	It is O.K. to be loud at a football game or when outside with friends, but it is not O.K. to be loud when at a movie or watching a play. It is appropriate to take off my hat at the dinner table.
Male/Female	Men don't normally call each other "boyfriends," whereas women can call each other "girlfriends" without social stigma. Men don't wear make-up, but many women do.
People You Are With at Home or in the Community	My friends may think it is funny when I burp out loud, but my parents or teachers will probably not think so. At a place of worship, it is typically not appropriate to rock and roll to the music while others are singing religious music.
School	It is considered appropriate to be clean when I go to school. It is polite not to speak out in class without the teacher calling on me first.
Work	I should not make noises that disturb my coworkers. I should not wear too much perfume or cologne at work, because it may make other people uncomfortable.

My Hidden Curriculum Diary – Blank

Age	
Place	
Male/Female	
People You Are With at Home or in the Community	
School	
Work	

Congratulations! We have finally come to the end of this workbook – but not the end of your journey. Change is hard and requires a lot of time and effort on your part. Keep this workbook when you are done, so you can refer to if you need to as the school year progresses. If you start to get anxious about your new school or new situations that you encounter, refer back to Chapter 3 and Chapter 10. It's O.K. to be anxious about new situations.

If you have difficulty finding strategies to help reduce your anxiety, talk with your parents, teachers, and other support staff at your new school. They may be able to help brainstorm some ideas with you. Chapter 9 is also a good chapter to review if you are struggling with making new friends at your new school.

I am very proud of all of the hard work that you have been doing to move to your new school. I wish you the best of luck in your adventure at your new school. Your new school is lucky to have you as a member of the school community!

GOOD LUCK!

References

Baker, J. (2003*). Social skills training for children and adolescents with Asperger Syndrome and social-communication problems.* Shawnee Mission, KS: Autism Asperger Publishing Company.

Buron, K. D., & Curtis, M. (2003). *The incredible 5-point scale: Assisting students with autism spectrum disorders in understanding social interactions and controlling their emotional responses.* Shawnee Mission, KS: Autism Asperger Publishing Company.

Buron, K. D. (2007). *A "5" could make me lose control! An activity-based method for evaluating and supporting highly anxious students.* Shawnee Mission, KS: Autism Asperger Publishing Company.

Buron, K. D. (2007). *A 5 is against the law! Social boundaries: Straight up! An honest guide for teens and young adults.* Shawnee Mission, KS: Autism Asperger Publishing Company.

Coucouvanis, J. (2005). *Super skills: A social skills group program for children with Asperger Syndrome, high-functioning autism and related challenges.* Shawnee Mission, KS: Autism Asperger Publishing Company.

Henry, S. A., & Myles, B. S. (2007). *Integrating best practices throughout the student's daily schedule: The Comprehensive Autism Planning System (CAPS) for individuals with Asperger Syndrome, autism and related disabilities.* Shawnee Mission, KS: Autism Asperger Publishing Company

Korin, E. S. H. (2006). *Asperger syndrome: An owner's manual: What you, your parents and your teachers need to know.* Shawnee Mission, KS: Autism Asperger Publishing Company.

Korin, E. S. H. (2007). *Asperger syndrome: An owner's manual 2 for older adolescents and adults: What you, your parents, and your employer need to know.* Shawnee Mission, KS: Autism Asperger Publishing Company.

Myles, B. S., Trautman, M. L., & Schelvan, R. L. (2004). *The hidden curriculum: Practical solutions for understanding unstated rules in social situations.* Shawnee Mission, KS: Autism Asperger Publishing Company.

Packer, A. J. (1997). *How rude! The teenager's guide to good manners, proper behavior, and not grossing people out.* Minneapolis, MN: Free Spirit Publishing Inc.

Paradiz, V. (2009). *The integrated self-advocacy ISA curriculum – A program for emerging self-advocates with autism spectrum and other conditions.* Shawnee Mission, KS: Autism Asperger Publishing Company,

Shore, S. (2004). *Ask and tell: Disclosure for people on the autism spectrum.* Shawnee Mission, KS: Autism Asperger Publishing Company.

Quotes on page 2 retrieved from http://www.wisdomquotes.com/cat_changegrowth.html

Appendix

5-Point Scale

1

I can handle this. I'm O.K.

2

This might make me feel uncomfortable,
but I will still try it.

3

This could make me very nervous. I might need someone
to help prepare me for this situation ahead of time.

4

This could make me feel sick to my stomach or
extremely nervous. I will need some help during
this situation to make it through.

5

There is no way that I will be able to handle
this situation.

Based on *The Incredible 5-Point Scale* by K. Buron and M. Curtis. (2003). Shawnee Mission, KS: Autism Asperger Publishing Company. Use with permission.

5-Point Scale Cards

Meeting new people	Eating in the lunchroom
Using a locker	Remembering my schedule
Remembering my locker combination	Math class
Communication arts (CA) class	Reading class
Science class	Social studies class

5-Point Scale Cards

Walking in the hallways	Staying organized
Tests	Homework
Teachers yelling at me	Exploratory class
School assembly	Not knowing what to say to other students
Being the new kid in school	Having a substitute teacher

5-Point Scale Cards

Being late for school	PE class
My schedule being changed	Noisy classrooms
Fire drills	Tornado drills
Group work in classrooms	Going to school
State assessments	MAP assessments

5-Point Scale Cards

A**PC

Autism Asperger Publishing Company
P.O. Box 23173
Shawnee Mission, Kansas 66283-0173
877-277-8254
www.asperger.net